Crochet

Learn to crochet
three great projects

Anne Akers Johnson

KLUTZ® creates activity books and other great stuff for kids ages 3 to 103. We began our corporate life in 1977 in a garage we shared with a Chevrolet Impala. Although we've outgrown that first office, Klutz galactic headquarters remains in Palo Alto, California, and we're still staffed entirely by real human beings. For those of you who collect mission statements, here's ours:

Create wonderful things
Be good • Have fun

Write Us
We would love to hear your comments regarding this or any of our books. We have many!

KLUTZ®
450 Lambert Avenue
Palo Alto, CA 94306
thefolks@klutz.com

All components manufactured in China. 112

Distributed in the UK by
Scholastic UK Ltd
Westfield Road
Southam, Warwickshire
England CV47 0RA

Distributed in Canada by
Scholastic Canada Ltd
604 King Street West
Toronto, Ontario
Canada M5V 1E1

Distributed in Australia by
Scholastic Australia Ltd
PO Box 579
Gosford, NSW
Australia 2250

Distributed in Hong Kong by
Scholastic Hong Kong Ltd
Suites 2001-2, Top Glory Tower
262 Gloucester Road
Causeway Bay, Hong Kong

ISBN: 978-0-545-67588-8
4 1 5 8 5 7 0 8 8 8

FSC
www.fsc.org
MIX
Paper from
responsible sources
FSC™ C113204

We make Klutz books using resources that have been approved by the Forest Stewardship Council™. This means the paper in this book comes exclusively from trees that have been grown and harvested responsibly.

Basics

Projects

Basics

In this section, you'll learn the basics of crochet. If you've never picked up a crochet hook before, this is the place to start. Take the time to make a small sample of each stitch. It's the best way to learn.

What comes with this book

This book comes with everything you need to start crocheting right away.

DK weight yarn

The yarn that comes with this book is DK (double knit) weight. It comes in two colors: teal and blue. There's more teal yarn, so you'll need to use this color to make the hat. You can make the flower and the jewelry bag out of either color.

4.0 mm crochet hook

This hook will work with both of the yarns that come with this book. When you're buying hooks, always look for the correct size in millimeters.

Ruler

There's a ruler printed on the inside front cover of this book.

Stitch markers

Use these when you want to mark the position of a particular stitch. You'll need them to make the hat.

Yarn needle

Use this special needle to sew your projects together.

You'll also need:

Scissors (small ones are fine)

Caring for your yarn

Both of these yarns are 100% viscose. If you want to clean a finished project, simply wash it by hand in cool water then lay it flat to dry. Don't put it in the dryer and never iron it.

Winding yarn

The yarn that comes with this book is wrapped into skeins. When your yarn comes this way (which it often does) you'll need to wrap it into a ball before you use it. If you try to crochet without doing this, you'll end up with a big, tangled mess.

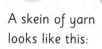

A skein of yarn looks like this:

Carefully pull the skein apart. You'll see that it's a big circle of yarn tied together at some point. Untie or cut the yarn that holds the skein together...

...then carefully drape the skein over the back of a chair as shown in the picture. This will keep it from tangling as you wind.

Hold the end of the yarn with your thumb, then wrap the yarn around two fingers about 10 times.

Take the yarn off your fingers, turn it and wrap in a different direction as shown in the picture.

Wind the yarn like this maybe 6 or 7 times...

...then turn the ball of yarn again and make a few more wraps in a different direction. Continue to wrap the yarn every which way to make a nice round ball.

Most yarn stores will wind your yarn free of charge. Be sure to ask.

9

How to hold your hands

Yarn hand

1 Hold the yarn in your **right** hand, about 6 inches (15 cm) from the end. Wrap the yarn over and around your **left** pinkie...

...up over your two middle fingers...

about 6 inches long

2 ...and behind your first finger, like so:

Next wrap the yarn down over your first finger...

Yarn hand

1 Hold the yarn in your **left** hand, about 6 inches (15 cm) from the end. Wrap the yarn over and around your **right** pinkie...

...up over your two middle fingers...

about 6 inches long

2 ...and behind your first finger, like so:

Next wrap the yarn down over your first finger...

...and pinch it between your thumb and second finger like this:

You should still have about 6 inches of yarn hanging down.

Working hand

Hold the hook in your **right** hand, like this:

 ...and pinch it between your thumb and second finger like this:

You should still have about 6 inches of yarn hanging down.

Working hand

Hold the hook in your **left** hand, like this:

The rest of the instructions are written for right-handed crocheters. Lefties, simply reverse the instructions to make them work for you.

Foundation chain

Once you know how to hold your hands, you're ready to start crocheting. Every project starts with a simple chain. Here's how you make one.

1 Hold the yarn in your left hand (lefties, in your right hand) as shown on page 10.

4 ...like this:

5 Pinch the bottom of the loop to hold it in place, then reach your hook up and pick up the yarn that runs down off your first finger.

— Pinch here.

7 ...like so:

8 Turn your hook so it faces up. You've just made one chain and are ready to make the next one.

12

2 Now lay your crochet hook on top of the yarn with the hook facing down.

3 Pull your hook down, toward yourself then back up to loop the yarn around the hook...

6 Turn your hook so it faces down and pull this yarn through the loop...

Don't be surprised if your first chain doesn't look just right. It takes a little practice before your stitches are neat and even like in the picture.

9 Repeat steps 5–8 until you've made as many stitches as you need.

Keep your loops a little loose. This is about the right size.

Single crochet

The first stitch you're going to learn is the single crochet. It's the shortest, simplest stitch.

Follow the directions on the next four pages to make a small practice piece. It's the best way to learn. You can keep this practice piece forever, or you can unravel it and reuse the yarn to make a project. Always work with fresh yarn when you're learning a new stitch.

1 To make a practice piece 12 stitches wide, start by making a foundation of **13 chain stitches.**

— 13 stitches

The first single crochet will go in the **second stitch** from your hook (it's purple in the picture).

3 ...so you have **two loops** on your hook. Perfect.

4 Pick up the yarn with your hook and pull it through **both loops** on your hook.

5 The last stitch can be a little tricky. If you pulled the first stitch of your foundation chain too tight, it will be hard to get your hook into it to make the last stitch.

If this happens, simply loosen the first stitch a bit so you can make the last stitch.

too tight

just right

Turning chain

At the end of every row, you have to make a **turning chain.** This is simply a chain that brings your work up to the height of the next row so that your edges stay nice and straight. The length of the chain is different for each stitch. For the single crochet, the turning chain is **1 chain stitch.**

2 Push your hook into the stitch and pick up the yarn like so:

Now pull the yarn through the **first loop** on your hook...

5 You'll be left with **one loop** and you've just finished your first single crochet.

The next stitch goes here.

Make a **single crochet** in the next stitch and in every stitch to the end of the row.

7 Count to be sure you have 12 stitches, then make **1 chain stitch** as the turning chain.

Now, without moving your hook, turn your work over so it's to the left of the hook again (lefties, to the right). Turn the page to see what this looks like.

Tension

One of the hardest things about learning to crochet is getting the tension right. Most beginners tend to crochet too tightly. To keep your stitches from pulling too tight, pinch the bottom of the loops you're working on to hold them in place as you pull the yarn through.

Pinch here.

Use the first finger of your working hand to guide the yarn on the hook as you work.

You'll learn more about tension, also called gauge, on page 30.

Counting stitches

To count your stitches, simply look at the top edge of your work. Every chain stitch represents a stitch.

1 2 3 4 5 6 7 8 9 10 11 12

It's a good idea to count the stitches at the end of each row when you're learning. It's easy to miss the last stitch.

Second row

The only difference between the first row of crochet and the second is where you place your hook in the stitch.

1 Check to be sure your crochet looks like the picture, then start the second row. You're going to skip the turning chain and make the first **single crochet** in the **second stitch** from the hook. It's purple in the picture.

turning chain

4 Now pull the yarn through the **two loops** to finish the single crochet as always.

5 Make a **single crochet** in the next stitch and in every stitch to the end of the row.

Push your hook under both loops of the stitch.

8 Work as many rows as it takes for you to feel comfortable with single crochet.

If you want to save your practice piece, you can cut the end and tie it off as shown in the next few steps. Otherwise, you can unravel your work and wind the yarn into a ball to use again.

Tying off

To tie off, cut the yarn so it's about 6 inches (15 cm) long, then pull it all the way through the last stitch.

6"

2 Push your hook under **both loops** of the stitch as shown.

Pick up the yarn and pull it through **both loops** of the stitch...

3 ...so you have **two loops** on your hook.

6 Before you make the turning chain, count to be sure you have 12 stitches. If you don't, you may have missed the last one. This is easy to do as it often rolls back a bit.

Make the last stitch here.

7 When you've finished the row, **chain 1** to make the turning chain. Turn your work so it's to the left of your hook and you're ready to start the next row.

Pull the end tight to tighten the knot.

Single crochet details

The foundation chain is always one stitch longer than the number of stitches you want in the first row.

The turning chain is one chain stitch.

On the second and all following rows, the first single crochet is made in the second stitch from your hook.

Half double crochet

This stitch is a little taller than the single crochet but it's just as easy. It makes a slightly softer, looser fabric than the single crochet does. It's used to make the flower.

You'll do best if you start a new practice piece to learn this stitch.

1 To make a practice piece 12 stitches wide, start by making a foundation of **14 chain stitches.**

5 Pick up the yarn again and pull it through **all three loops** on your hook.

6 You just made your first half double crochet. It will look like this:

Your next stitch goes right here.

Now wrap the yarn around your hook again and make a **half double crochet** in the next stitch and in every stitch to the end of the row.

8 Skip the turning chain and make a **half double crochet** in the **third stitch** from your hook, then in every stitch to the end of the row.

turning chain

9 Count to be sure you have 12 stitches. If you have too few, you probably missed the last one. If you have too many, go back to step 8 to be sure you made the first stitch in the right place.

The last stitch goes here.

2 Wrap the yarn around your hook one time as shown.

The first half double crochet will go in the **third stitch** from your hook (it's purple in the picture).

 Your first stitch goes here.

3 Push your hook into the stitch, pick up the yarn and pull it back through the **first loop** on your hook...

4 ...so you have **three loops** on your hook.

7 Count to be sure you have 12 stitches, then **chain 2** to make the turning chain. Turn your work over and you're ready to start the next row.

Half double crochet details

The foundation chain is always two stitches longer than the number of stitches you want in the first row.

The turning chain is two chain stitches.

On the second and all following rows, the first half double crochet is made in the third stitch from your hook.

10 Crochet as many rows as it takes to feel comfortable with the half double crochet. When you're finished, tie this piece off or unravel it and wind the yarn into a ball to use again.

Double crochet

This stitch is even taller than the half double crochet. It's the most commonly used stitch, so it's important that you learn how to make it.

Once again, start a new practice piece to learn this stitch.

The double crochet is different from the other stitches you've learned so far. Here the turning chain counts as the first double crochet. So if you're making a piece 12 stitches wide, you'll actually only make 11 double crochets. This will make more sense once you work through the steps.

4 ...so you have **three loops** on your hook.

5 Pick up the yarn again and pull it through the **first two loops** on your hook.

6 You'll have **two loops** left on your hook.

9 Count to be sure you have 12 stitches. Count the first 3 chain stitches in the row as the first double crochet. This will be followed by 11 double crochets.

Chain 3 to make the turning chain, then turn your work over.

10 Skip the turning chain and the next stitch. Make a **double crochet** in the **fifth stitch** from your hook, then in every stitch to the end of the row.

Your first stitch goes here.

This is a little different from the stitches you've learned so far.

1 To make a practice piece 12 stitches wide, start by making a foundation of **14 chain stitches.**

 2 Wrap the yarn around your hook **one time**.

The first double crochet will go in the **fourth stitch** from your hook.

The first stitch goes here.

3 Push your hook into the stitch, pick up the yarn and pull it back through the **first loop** on your hook...

 7 Pick up the yarn once more and pull it through the **last two loops.**

 8 You've just made a double crochet. It will look like this:

Wrap the yarn around your hook again and make a **double crochet** in the next stitch and in every stitch to the end of the row.

On your first row, these 3 chain stitches count as the first double crochet.

Note

The last double crochet goes in the top stitch of the turning chain that started the previous row.

here will e a little ap here.

Don't be surprised to see a little gap between the turning chain and the double crochet next to it. This is right.

 11 Crochet as many rows as it takes to feel comfortable with the double crochet. When you're finished, tie this piece off or unravel it and wind the yarn into a ball to use again.

Double crochet details

The foundation chain is always two stitches longer than the number of stitches you want in the first row.

The turning chain is three chain stitches long and counts as your first double crochet.

On the second and all following rows, the first double crochet is made in the fifth stitch from your hook.

Triple crochet

This is the tallest stitch yet. You'll probably never make a whole piece out of triple crochet, so don't worry too much about remembering how to start and end the rows just right.

Start a new practice piece to learn this stitch.

1 To make a practice piece 12 stitches wide, start by making a foundation of **15 chain stitches.**

5 Now pick up the yarn again and pull it through the **first two loops** on your hook.

6 You'll have **three loops** left on your hook.

7 Pick up the yarn again and pull it through the **next two loops**...

11 Count to be sure you have 12 stitches. The first 4 chain stitches in the row count as the first triple crochet. It will be followed by 11 triple crochets. **Chain 4** to make the turning chain, then turn your work over.

12 Skip the turning chain and the next stitch. Make a **triple crochet** in the **sixth stitch** from your hook, then in every stitch to the end of the row.

The first stitch goes here.

22

2 Wrap the yarn around your hook **two times.** The first triple crochet will go in the **fifth** stitch from your hook.

The first stitch goes here.

3 Push your hook into this stitch, pick up the yarn and pull it through the **first loop**...

4 ...so you have **four loops** on your hook.

8 ...so there are just **two loops** left on your hook.

9 Finally pull the yarn through the **last two loops**...

10 ...and you've finished a triple crochet.

Make a **triple crochet** in the next stitch and in every stitch to the end of the row.

These 4 stitches count as the first triple crochet.

Note

The last triple crochet goes in the top stitch of the turning chain that started the previous row.

The last stitch goes here.

13 Crochet as many rows as it takes to feel comfortable with the triple crochet. When you're finished, tie this piece off or unravel it and wind the yarn into a ball to use again.

Triple crochet details

The foundation chain is always three stitches longer than the number of stitches you want in the first row.

The turning chain is four chain stitches long and counts as the first triple crochet.

On the second and all following rows, the first triple crochet is made in the sixth stitch from the hook.

Slip stitch

The slip stitch is used to join rounds or to move the yarn from one place in your work to another without cutting it. While it may not seem like much on its own, it's a simple little stitch that makes bigger things possible.

1 When a slip stitch is called for, simply push your hook into the stitch indicated in the pattern....

2 ...pick up the yarn and pull it through all of the loops on your hook...

3 ...so you're left with one loop. It's that easy.

Tying off

One of the last things you do when you finish a crochet project is tie the yarn off. This is done the same way no matter what stitch you're using.

1 After you've finished the last stitch, cut the yarn so it's about 6 inches (15 cm) long, then pick it up with your hook and pull it all the way through the last loop.

2 Pull the yarn to make a nice snug knot and you're finished.

Adding yarn

Sooner or later you're going to run out of yarn in the middle of a project. Or you'll want to change colors. In both cases, you'll need to know how to add yarn. While it's possible to add yarn in the middle of a row, it's always better to do it at the end of a row if you can. Here's how:

Work the last stitch until there are just two loops left on your hook (three if it's a half double crochet). Be sure that there are at least 6 inches (15-cm) of the old yarn remaining.

Pull the new yarn through the remaining loops to finish the stitch. Leave a 6-inch (15-cm) tail on the new yarn as well.

If you're in the middle of a row, simply continue to crochet using the new yarn.

If you're at the end of a row, make your turning chain with the new yarn...

...then continue to crochet using the new yarn.

Sewing seams

Several of the projects in this book need to be sewn together. There are a lot of different ways to do this but a simple whip stitch will work well for all of the projects. When you're sewing your crochet together, be sure to use a yarn needle like the one that comes with this book.

Always leave a 6-inch (15-cm) tail on your sewing-up yarn so you can weave the end into your work later. You'll learn how to do this on the next page.

Thread some yarn onto your needle, then pull it almost all the way through the two layers that you're joining. Tie a nice tight knot as shown.

Now make simple whip stitches by pushing your needle up from the bottom to the top, stitching through both layers.

When you're finished, make one more stitch and push your needle through it to make a knot.

Weaving your yarn in

At the end of every project, you'll have at least a couple of loose ends of yarn hanging off. Hide these ends by weaving them into your work.

Whenever you start a project or add yarn, be sure to leave a 6-inch (15-cm) tail of yarn. This gives you plenty of yarn to thread onto your needle and weave into your work.

Thread the loose yarn onto your yarn needle and weave it through some stitches on the back of your work. Weave in at least 3 inches (8 cm), then trim the yarn short.

Blocking your work

What is blocking?

Blocking is simply a way to get the final shape of your project just right and to smooth out uneven stitches a bit. You do it after you've finished crocheting your project.

When to block?

Most of the projects in this book don't need to be blocked. Projects made of acrylic yarn don't need to be blocked. But if you've crocheted something using a natural fiber and it isn't shaped quite right, blocking will help.

How to block:

There are a lot of different ways to block your work. Here's an easy way that works especially well for small projects.

2–3"

1. Lay your finished work down on a thick towel or a couple of towels laid on top of each other. You can block a project before it's assembled or after.

2. Now hold a steaming iron a couple of inches (at least 5 cm) away from your work and steam the whole thing. Never let the iron touch the yarn.

3. Set the iron aside and gently smooth your crocheted piece to shape it. It sometimes helps to pin your work to the towel after you've steamed it so that it holds its shape as it dries.

Gauge

When you start looking at crochet patterns, you'll see that they all specify a gauge. Gauge is simply the number of stitches per inch of crochet. Measuring your gauge is important when you're making something that has to be sized just right, like a hat. If you crochet too tightly, your hat will be too small. Too loosely, and it will be too big.

Checking your gauge is easy. Always check your gauge over 4 inches (10 cm). Because the edges of your work can be a little uneven, make a sample piece about 5 inches (13 cm) wide and a couple of rows long. Be sure to work in the stitch specified by the pattern. Lay your work flat, place a ruler on top of it and count the stitches across a span of 4 inches in the middle of a row.

The yarn that comes with this book has a gauge of 4 single crochets per inch. That means you should count 16 stitches over 4 inches (10 cm).

If you have fewer than 16 stitches, try working a little tighter OR try using a slightly smaller crochet hook.

If you have more than 16 stitches, your gauge is a little tight. Try working your stitches a little looser OR try using a slightly larger crochet hook.

Remember, for most of the projects in this book, getting close to the right gauge is good enough.

It's not important that your gauge be exactly right for any project except the hat. Still, it's a good idea to check your gauge as you're learning, just to be sure you're on the right track.

Buying more yarn

The first time you walk into a yarn store, you may feel a little overwhelmed. You'll see yarn in different weights, different materials, different textures, not to mention all the different colors. **Don't panic**. Finding the right yarn is easier than it seems. Yarn comes in a variety of weights (sport, DK, worsted, bulky, etc.). Each weight has a different gauge and will be worked with a different size hook. When you're buying yarn for a project, look for something that is the same weight as the yarn your pattern calls for. This should get you to the right gauge. Here are some more tips for finding the right yarn.

Tips for buying yarn

✳ All of the projects in this book are made with DK (double knit) weight yarn. Look for this weight when you shop for more yarn.

✳ Yarn stores usually organize their yarn by weight, so you can simply tell the salesperson what you're looking for and they'll point you in the right direction.

✳ Most patterns call for a specific brand of yarn. Don't let this throw you. You can use any yarn that's the same weight as the yarn called for.

✳ If you're still not sure what to buy, just ask. People who work in yarn stores are used to helping people find the right yarn. Even experienced crocheters ask for help. Really.

Reading labels

The information printed on yarn labels varies from yarn to yarn. If you're lucky, you'll find something like this:

This tells you that the yarn is DK weight.

This number tells you what size crochet hook to use with the yarn.

The **8 UK** and **US 6** tell knitters what size needles to use.

· Some labels will show a picture of a crochet hook with the correct size noted. Easy.

· If you only see knitting-needle size noted, you're probably still ok. When a 4.0 mm knitting needle is called for, look for a crochet hook of the same size.

Real-world crochet

Once you've worked through the projects in this book, you're ready to take on just about any crochet pattern. Even the most complex stitch combinations are made up of the basic stitches you've already learned.

When you pick up other books or patterns, you'll see that they're written in a kind of crochet code. There will be a lot of abbreviations. There will be very few full sentences. You'll probably find it all a little intimidating. **Don't**.

Remember: You know the basics. And just about every pattern will include a guide telling you what each abbreviation stands for. Just in case you need them, you'll find a list of common abbreviations to the right.

beg	beginning		sc	single crochet
ch	chain		sk	skip
dc	double crochet		sl st	slip stitch
dec	decrease		sp	space
hdc	half double crochet		st	stitch
inc	increase		tog	together
lp	loop		tr	triple crochet
rnd	round		yo	yarn over*

* **Yarn over** is simply another way of telling you to wrap the yarn around your hook.

Hook placement

You've learned to crochet by pushing your hook under both loops of each stitch. You'll find some patterns that ask you to work into the front or back loop only. The picture to the right will show you what this means.

Try working some practice rows to see what it looks like when you push your hook through a different part of the stitch.

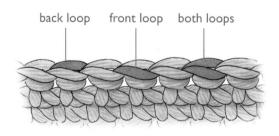

back loop   front loop   both loops

Crochet in the UK

The crochet terms used in this book are from the United States. If you're buying patterns or books in the UK, you'll find a whole different set of terms. Don't worry. The stitches are the same, it's just the names that are different.

Here's a quick cheat sheet to help you translate.

US	UK
single crochet	double crochet (dc)
half double crochet	half treble crochet (htr)
double crochet	treble crochet (tr)
triple crochet	double treble crochet (dtr)
slip stitch	slip stitch (sl st)

Measurements in the UK are always metric.

One last bit of advice

If you ask three different crocheters how to do something, you may get three different answers. Don't be put off by this. If someone shows you a different way of doing something, give it a try. It might just work better for you.

Remember, if it works, it's right.

Projects

Once you've worked through the basics of crochet and feel pretty comfortable with the different stitches, you're ready to make one of the projects. The first two are the quickest and the easiest to complete. Start with one of these and you'll be an expert by the time you get to the hat.

Jewelry Roll

This is the perfect
project to make first.
It's easy and beautiful.
Crochet the first one
for yourself, then make
more to give as gifts.

If you know how to
make a single crochet,
you're ready to start.

What You Need

4.0 mm crochet hook

50 yards (45 m) of DK yarn

yarn needle

This is a great time to work on getting your gauge right. The gauge for the yarn that comes with this book is 4 single crochets per inch (2.5 cm). So if you're on target, your jewelry roll will measure about 5 inches (13 cm) across. For this project close is good enough.

1 Start by making a chain of 21 stitches. Then make a **single crochet** in the second stitch from the hook. It's darker in the picture.

The first single crochet goes here.

2 Perfect. Now make a **single crochet** in the next stitch and in every stitch to the end of the row.

The next single crochet goes here.

3 Count to be sure you have 20 stitches, then **chain 1** to make a turning chain.

4 Turn your work over. Repeat the instructions in the box until your piece is 7 inches (18 cm) long. It doesn't have to be exact.

The first stitch goes here.

- Make a **single crochet** in the second stitch from the hook, and then in every stitch to the end of the row.
- Count to be sure you have 20 stitches.
- **Chain 1.**
- Turn your work over.

Now you're ready to assemble your roll. It's easy.

7 Lay your work down flat so that the long end of yarn is at the bottom. Fold the bottom edge up 2 inches (5 cm) to make a little pocket.

long end

2"

5

Your jewelry roll will look like this:

7"

6

Cut the end of the yarn so it's about 10 inches (25 cm) long, and pull it all the way through the last stitch to tie off.

10"

8

Thread the long end of yarn onto your yarn needle and use a whip stitch to sew the edges of the folded-up pocket together.

9 Knot your yarn and weave it into the inside of the pocket.

Thread your needle with another piece of yarn and sew up the other side of the pocket in the same way.

Weave all the loose ends of yarn into your work.

Forgot how to weave in? Go to page 28 for a reminder.

11

Turn your bag over so the pocket is face down. Use your crochet hook to weave the tie through a couple of rows of crochet at the very center of your piece.

12

Your jewelry roll will look something like this:

10 Now you're ready to make the tie. To do this, simply make a chain about 15 inches (38 cm) long. It can be the same color as your roll, or it can be something different.

Tie it off when it's long enough.

Make a bag for your glasses

Simply start with a foundation chain that's a little longer than your glasses are wide. Work until your piece is as long as it needs to be to make a deep-enough pocket and a long-enough flap.

The bag in the picture started with a foundation chain of 24 stitches and made a bag about 6 inches (15 cm) wide. The flap is just long enough to reach the bottom of the pocket.

Or a bag for your crochet hooks

This bag was a 6-inch (15-cm) square before the pocket was folded up.

13 Pull the ends of your tie really tight, then cut them short. Your bag is ready to use!

Cut here.

Flower

*This pretty little flower
is quick and easy to
make. Sew it on a hat,
pin it to your jacket or
tie it to your flip-flops.*

*You'll need to know the
half double, double and
triple crochet stitches
to make this project.*

What You Need

4.0 mm crochet hook

7 yards (6.5 m) of yarn

yarn needle

You can make the flower using either of the yarns that come with this book.

1 Start by making a chain of 6 stitches. Next you're going to join the ends of the chain. To do this, push your hook through the first stitch...

2 ...pick up the yarn and pull it through both loops on your hook.

3 Good. Now chain 3.

43

4 Make **14 double crochets** right into the center of the ring...

Tip

Crochet right over the short end of yarn so you don't have to weave it in later.

center of ring

7 Check to be sure your flower looks like the picture. **Chain 1.**

5 ...like so:

Push your hook into this space.

Next you're going to join your work into a complete circle with a **slip stitch**. To do this, poke your hook into the space between that string of 3 chains and the first double crochet...

6 ...pick up the yarn and pull it through both loops on your hook.

8 Now you're ready to start the first petal.

The next 3 stitches go here.

In the next stitch, make these three stitches:

· 1 half double crochet
· 1 double crochet
· 1 triple crochet

9 Good. That's half a petal. Now make the other half.

The next 3 stitches go here.

In the next stitch make:

· 1 triple crochet
· 1 double crochet
· 1 half double crochet

10 To finish your petal, **chain 1.**

11 Now make a **slip stitch** into the next stitch.

Make a slip stitch right here.

Slip stitch reminder

Push your hook under the next stitch, pick up the yarn and pull it all the way through both loops on your hook.

12 Repeat steps 7–11 to make a total of 5 petals.

Make a **slip stitch** into the last stitch...

Tie a flower to your flip-flop...

...or onto the strap of your bag.

13 ...then cut the end of the yarn so it's about 6 inches (15 cm) long. Pull it all the way through the last stitch to tie off.

Weave the loose ends of yarn into the back of your flower. Very nice.

Hat

This hat, with its pretty scalloped trim, is actually quite easy to make. It's worked in the round, so there's no seam to sew up. Make the hat all one color, or choose a different color for the scallop.

You'll need to know both single and double crochet.

What You Need

4.0 mm crochet hook

115 yards (104 m) of the teal DK yarn

stitch marker

yarn needle

The hat is the one project in this book where gauge matters. If you crochet too tightly, your hat may turn out too small. Too loosely, and it may turn out too big.

The correct gauge for this hat is 13–14 double crochets over 4 inches (10 cm). Turn to page 30 if you need help checking your gauge.

1 Start by making a chain of 4 stitches. Join the ends by making a **slip stitch** in the first stitch...

2 ...like so:

3 You'll have a little ring of yarn. **Chain 3.**

4 Now make **9 double crochets** right into the center of the ring.

center of ring

Keep the short end of yarn close to your work and crochet right over it so you don't have to weave it in later.

You'll be making increases to your hat over the next five rounds. This simply means you'll be adding stitches. Find a quiet place where you can crochet uninterrupted while you're working these rounds. Increasing isn't difficult, but you have to count your stitches carefully as you work.

Make 2 double crochets into this space.

5 Find one of your stitch markers and slip it onto the stitch that's on your hook. Check the picture to be sure you've got it right.

Now make **2 double crochets** into the space between that first string of chains and the first double crochet.

If you can't find your stitch markers, a small safety pin will work just as well.

6 It will look like this:

There should be 9 stitches between your hook and the stitch marker.

Now make **2 double crochets** in the next stitch and in every stitch around. Stop when you get to the stitch marker.

7 You've just finished the second round. Starting with the stitch with your marker on it, count to be sure you have 20 stitches.

8 Move your marker to the loop on your hook, then repeat the stitches in the purple box all the way around.

Make a double crochet here.

- **1 double crochet** in the next stitch
- **2 double crochets** in the following stitch

9 Stop when you get to your marker. Count to be sure you have 30 stitches now.

10 Move your marker to the loop on your hook and start the 4th round. Repeat the stitches in the box all the way around. They're different from the last round.

Make a double crochet here.

- 1 double crochet in the next 2 stitches
- 2 double crochets in the following stitch

11 Stop when you come to your marker. Count to be sure you have 40 stitches now.

Tip

The last stitch in every round should have 2 double crochets in it. If it doesn't, you probably miscounted. You'll have to unravel your work to find your mistake.

14 Move your marker to the loop on your hook, and start the last round of increases. Repeat the stitches in the box all the way around.

Make a double crochet in this stitch.

- 1 double crochet in the next 4 stitches
- 2 double crochets in the following stitch

15 Stop when you come to your marker. You should have 60 stitches.

12 Move your marker to the loop on your hook and start the 5th round. Repeat the stitches in the box all the way around.

Make a double crochet in this stitch.

- **1 double crochet** in the next 3 stitches
- **2 double crochets** in the following stitch

13 Stop when you come to your marker. You should have 50 stitches.

16 You've finished the hard part. Move your marker down a row so it's out of your way but marks the end of the round. Make a **double crochet** in every stitch around...

Move your stitch marker down a row.

17 ...and around. Stop when your hat is a half inch (1.25 cm) short of long-enough. About 7 inches (18 cm) will be right for most people. Stop more-or-less in line with your stitch marker.

stitch marker

18 You're ready to start the scalloped edge. If you want the trim to be a different color, add new yarn on the next stitch (see page 26). Make a **single crochet** in the next stitch.

Make a single crochet right here.

19 Skip a stitch, then make **5 double crochets** in the next one.

Make 5 double crochets in this stitch.

22 When you get back to the beginning of the round, skip a stitch and make a **slip stitch** in the next one.

23 Cut your yarn so it's about 6 inches (15 cm) long and pull it all the way through the last stitch to tie off. Weave all the loose ends of yarn into your work. Beautiful!

20 Look at the picture to be
sure your scallop looks right.
Repeat the stitches in the box
to work the scallop
all the way around.

- Skip a stitch.
- Make a single crochet
  in the next one.
- Skip a stitch.
- Make 5 double crochets
  in the next one.

21 Your scalloped edge
will look like this:

To make the
trim a different
color, add a new color
of yarn as you make the
single crochet in step 18.
Go to page 26 if you
don't remember how
to do this.

thanks to everyone!

Book design
Keeli McCarthy

Production design
Maria Corrales

Art direction
Kate Paddock
Jill Turney

Technical illustration
Vally Hennings
Darwen Hennings

Decorative illustration
Keeli McCarthy

Calligraphy
Rosemary Woods

Photography
Katrine Naleid
Peter Fox
Joseph Quever
Judi Swinks

Watercolor
Liz Hutnick

Crochet consultant
Donna Swenson

Production Editor
Jen Mills

Sourcing
Paula Hannigan

Special thanks to
Sylvia Reader
Megan Smith
Laura Young
Laurie Campbell
Kathy Harrington
Georgia Herzog
Patty Morris
Rachelle Adams
Hollis Bischoff
and all the new
crocheters at Klutz

Boxed Kit Team
Maria Corrales
Kelly Beltramo
Madeleine Robins
Armin Bautista
David Avidor
With thanks to
Kathleen Campisano
Anne Klimpl
Annette Hughes